David,
Thank you for helping me find
so many of these words.

—Clem...

THE
WALMART
REPUBLIC

MONGREL EMPIRE PRESS
NORMAN, OKLAHOMA, UNITED STATES OF AMERICA

Norman, Oklahoma, USA
2014

FIRST EDITION, 2014

The Walmart Republic 2014
by Quraysh Ali Lansana & Christopher Stewart

ISBN 978-0-9903204-0-1

Cover Images:
Puzzling Land © Gay Pasley & John Jernigan, 2014

Big Tex Burning © Christian Bradford
Use via a Wikimedia Commons Generic 2.0 license.

MONGREL EMPIRE PRESS
NORMAN, OK

ONLINE CATALOGUE: WWW.MONGRELEMPIRE.ORG

This publisher is a proud member of

COUNCIL OF LITERARY MAGAZINES & PRESSES
www.clmp.org

Book Design: Mongrel Empire Press using iWork Pages

CONTENTS

ACKNOWLEDGEMENTS

Grateful acknowledgement from both authors is made to the
editors of the following publications in which versions of these
poems originally appeared:

Vice Versa
Coffeehouse Poets Quarterly
This Land Press
Poets and Artists
Gazelle Poets Anthology
Southside Rain/Third World Press
Bum Rush the Page: A Def Poetry Jam/Broadway Books
*Role Call: A Generational Anthology of Social and Political Black
Literature and Art/Third World Press*
Red Truck Review
World Literature Today
Oklahoma Poems . . . and Their Poets/Mezcalita Press, LLC
reluctant minivan/Living Arts Press
After Hours

Thanks to Dr. Jeanetta Calhoun Mish, Adrian Matejka, Mark Turcotte and Georgia A. Popoff for their insights on these poems. Additional thanks to Angela Jackson, Elise Paschen, and Nathan Brown for their kind words. Also thanks to the Evanston Public Library, Guild Complex Literary Center (where this book was conceived in the early 1990's), the Red Earth MFA Program at Oklahoma City University, Scott Gregory/*This Land Press* and Amy Wilson/*Red Truck Review*. Thanks also to the students of my Spring 2014 Honors Composition II class (Natasha Banks, Jennifer Fordjour, Glafira Gonzalez & Candis Short).

Special thanks to Dr. Raymond Merlock, a professor of journalism, fine arts and communication studies at the University of South Carolina Upstate, who in a 1983 University of Oklahoma classroom dropped the bomb of wisdom that is this book's title.

Extra special thanks to Christopher Stewart, who I met at an open mic in 1990 and has been family ever since. Over the years I have called you Slicketyhead and Booga, but your first name is always Brotha.

Thanks to Guild Complex for giving me a home and a voice for so many years. Also, thanks to Edward Pinkowski, who proved to me that it is truly never too late.

Thanks to my brothers and sisters. We were seven on a journey. Though time and distance has drawn us apart, I am with you in these pages. Special thanks to Claire Dougherty Stewart, who has seen me through folly and flounder, yet never wavered. I hope I have been as strong for you as you have for me.

Quraysh Ali Lansana, I would say that I am grateful beyond what simple words can express, but you would, of course, refuse to let me abandon language. You never have. You are truth. Thank you, brother. Thank you.

CS

THE
WALMART
REPUBLIC

I.

BUICK

In the November dusk, a rusted white Buick
wrecks the quiet of West Diversey Parkway.

A tattered, dime store American flag
hangs from the jagged hole
where the antennae used to be.
The hulk turns left on Austin Avenue

heading north towards Wisconsin
where the snow already covers the cornfields
in Iowa County, harvested in October,
left to dream of seeds in May.

The slow sound of breathing metal
wheezes in the autumn air
as he pulls out of sight. We get home

watch Thursday night sitcoms,
and get on with the work
of fattening up for winter.

CS

JAMESTOWN, NY

After the separation, a man checks in
to the Holiday Inn in Jamestown, New York.
There are plenty on vacancies, most of
the business having left with the last of the furniture
factories, only him in an empty hotel room
with pay per view movies and plenty of clean ashtrays.
He thinks that if he could hear
anything from this room, it would be the wind
off of Lake Erie, cold even in June,
blowing down Foundry Street, past the abandoned
rail yards where, according to an old guidebook
only half a generation ago, over 500 tons of couches
and e-z sleep recliners were loaded everyday, bound
for sturdy, middle class neighborhoods in places
where most things remained constant. He thinks
about the kind of space this kind of dying
offers, and how they hated each other more
and more as the house grew emptier,
how, on that last night, they didn't even
have a mattress to sleep on, and how the wind, cold
even in summer, would always fill the empty
spaces: a warehouse in Jamestown, the distance between
two lovers' bodies, rooms without furniture.

CS

14

FOR WATER

Rain in Dublin. Two women in bikinis posing with a bottle of
Spanish champagne in an antique bathtub placed in the middle
of Grafton Street. A midday crowd of stockbrokers and
students slice a path around the light stands and boom flashes
on the sidewalk, noticing for a minor urban moment, then
moving on to the business of the day, perhaps a beat slower
than we did this morning getting off the train in Galway,
pressing with the rest of the tourists around the elderly woman
as she struggled through the exit, her feet swollen with
diabetes, her back bent with weary. Water

finds its level. In doing so, can rot away the foundation of a
four bedroom house in rural Pennsylvania as children, then
grandchildren are raised, births and deaths attended, mysteries
of small things appreciated in the sanguine, plodding routine of
family life. Years later, a great-nephew receives the news as he
readies the house for sale: corrosion up the masonry walls,
floor joists buckling with the burden of hidden moisture, load
bearing brick made porous with decay, the very heart of the
home compromised. "It can't be!" the young man exclaims, "I
knew this house, My uncles were handy. There were never
floods, visible leaks. It was a dry, warm place. We were always
welcome here." And with all of this,

the simple beginnings of time and topographical circumstance,
birthing great rivers that begin as infinitesimal streams, cutting
paths through tremendous canyons, pouring silt and soil over
desiccated plains, creasing a trickle through a seam in my
umbrella to puddle in the nape of my neck, in Dublin on a
rainy Friday, finding my way home.

CS

THE WARBLERS

"If they knew it was March," I say to Mrs. Munoz,
"the warblers wouldn't sing." It is Saturday
on Ridgeway Avenue. First thaw. Filigree of ice
droop from the miniature evergreens that keep guard
around her bungalow like tired, tiny centurians
who have seen a hundred tours, and no longer care
the difference between home and duty.

She rakes soggy November leaves into a slush pile
over the curb. Her husband said it's never too early
to start. I remember a Christmas funeral, how diabetes
took its time with him, until a gangrenous toe fell away,
then a foot, then his legs. She buried a third of a man.
"What you don't know, young man," she says,
is that they *do* know it's March.
And that is precisely why they sing."

Usually, I find my wife asleep. I follow her
there with wine and tobacco on my breath
on nights when there is nothing between us
but the sound of an engine idling in the distance.
The promise of something even and steady
sifting an unlikely chorus from it all.

CS

THE SUIT

The old man carefully lays a dark blue suit
over the counter at the dry cleaners. As Mrs. Kim
busies herself inspecting it, she speaks to him
in a mildly awkward, cheerful voice of someone
who learned English later in life. "How are you?"
she asks. "How your wife?"

"She passed away yesterday," the old man replies.

Mrs. Kim's eyes rise slowly from the fabric
to meet his. She is old as well, her body
crooked from years over a stitching machine.
The garment carousel whirs on its serpentine track.
Work shirts and cocktail dresses filled with light
and air mingle in the space above us. A late
summer sun sifts through the dust that mottles
the shop windows, laying a patchwork
of light on the scuffed linoleum floor, like gossamer
through the apostles in the clerestory windows
at Chartres, where my sister and I
wandered with the pilgrims and the tourists
that difficult summer, her at the end
of her marriage, me already with the knowing
what would become of my only child, undisturbed
and innocent in the deep dark of transition.

"May I have this suit back by Tuesday morning?"

A delivery truck gears down on Asbury Avenue, rattling
the shop door. Something rustles
behind a fitting room curtain. "Yes.

And no price for you, Mr. Lewis," she says.
"You already pay."

CS

17

MARRIED

On my wedding night, after our lovemaking
a brown recluse emerged from the sanding dust
to bite me on the wrist, a few inches above
my wedding band. She'd been saving it up
for months no doubt, outraged at the intrusion
of us, the carpenters and dry wall crews
laying waste to her nest as the new house was readied.

For weeks, the tissue numbed, burned slightly
when I reached for necessary things: a coffee cup,
a bar of soap, my new wife's breasts.

And for all of this I said nothing,
the business between the spider and me.

CS

OUTSIDE IN THE MIDDLE

There are plenty of beasts about, in early dawn up French Mountain. Not an ideal time for a seven mile run. Still, he had to clear his head of it, the taste of wine and cigarettes on her breath, the swirling sameness of their disagreements, which over the years have become the collective shape of them, like a familiar constellation guiding sailors across vast oceans, to ports known for commerce and carnality. In a few days, the men will be penniless and return, as they always do, to the sea. Until they grew exhausted with it, and made love on an aging mattress as the grey owls murmured through the mayblossoms and scots pines.

Not that it's easy in this light, when the night shapes loiter on the slope face, challenging the urgency of the oncoming day. The lightscape of a dream. Still, the matter would be settled soon enough. He turns south down a river road, which narrows gradually until, after the second mile, the tire ruts shallow and fade into what becomes little more than a pebble rock path, and the last filigree of new sunlight is lost in a canopy of birch and wild oak. The first advantage in any negotiation is location. Of this he is certain. Blood surges though his quadriceps. The river the sound of breaking glass below. Years swirl in the high mountain air. Some will be left there, others reclaimed by the broadleaf forest, which has cleared its agenda for this morning's meeting, in the half space between night and day.

CS

AN ENDING

As we round an inlet past Sturgeon Bay
two piping plovers cried warnings, enough
to call a nearby nest, or keep away
from a Cooper's hawk that shot from the bluff
to take one of the plovers as it flew
above the water's edge, and drowned the bird
in a tide pool, between two rocks. We knew
of the quick work hawks make of these things, heard
sound before dying before. How could we
then have prepared for the stubborn silence
of an underwater end? Now unfree,
we railed against it, though the violence
fueled our reaching that night before the fire.
Flesh ages, yet the body still desires.

CS

THE FIX IT MAN

For Craig Nakamoto

There are scattered moments, the first memories,
the ones that came after. The cool distance of him
in a tee shirt on Granville Avenue in July. He made
geometry out of decades, perfect circles,
and the occasional hypotenuse for you
from everyday things, even terrible things
he knew you had to understand.

When the frenzied mourning ends
and a familiar ache unfolds
as a January afternoon, do not be afraid.
In time it turns into those first times
when your eyes began to see. In time

the mysteries of circuitry, the impossible innards
of common knowledge, the way the slow river
behind his garage never made a sound, and he
more than anyone else, understood why.

My friend, I am empty handed for you.
I have only this: take the Blue Line from Clark Street.
Transfer to the Pulaski Avenue bus at Irving Park.
Walk north. Do this at morning
or at dusk. Forget for a moment
what lies between.

I will be with you there, with my own father,
alone, as men sometimes are.

CS

II.

BIBLE BELTED: FAITH

i harbor reasons
to kill. pain, history
& blood. don't know
why i have not.

QAL

BIBLE BELTED: COMMUNION

did not know
black folks could be
catholic until i moved
to chicago. i was twenty-five.

QAL

BIBLE BELTED: FOUND ONE

oklahoma the birthplace
of will rogers garth brooks
toby keith sam walton

QAL

BIBLE BELTED: FOUND TWO

oklahoma the birthplace
of the dawes act   tulsa race riot
the reservation   a 900 ft white jesus

QAL

BIBLE BELTED: GOOD NEWS

the evidence of things
not seen i believe. it's
what i have that is
unbelievable: trail of tears
revisited yearly, sam walton
worship. niggas the evil
root & cash crop.

QAL

29

BIBLE BELTED: HISTORY

okie white men
are a curious herd.
never sure if cowboy
or cracker. skin coated
in dust from 1830 or 1921
hard to tell. they grow
whiter with age.

QAL

BIBLE BELTED: MATH

Pro-Black doesn't mean anti-anything.
—El Hajj Malik El-Shabazz (Malcolm X)

there are at least twenty-seven
white people i love. i counted.

four from high school
five from undergraduate

years, maybe three from grad
school (one gay=bonus points)

and an assortment of compelling
melanin-deprived miscreants

in chicago and countrywide.
two brothas in the afterlife

remain why i add rather than
subtract.

QAL

III.

DALLAS, 1978

For some, memory is a crowded construction site.
They pause with their children, and speak of what will be,
marvel at the tower cranes swinging steel beams like toys
in the still summer sky, which is at once shapeless,
and formed. Limitless, and lined.

Others see what was lost, histories in alleyways and fried fish
joints, a bramble of storefronts where one could buy orange
juice and cigarettes, Mexican incense and Polish sausage.

When my brother split his knee on the Peak Street
sidewalk, we thought the world would end. I picked
the glass out of the wide cut and wrapped the injury
in my tee shirt. In solidarity, he took his shirt off, too.
We made the best of it, belting out 99 Bottles of Beer
on the Wall as we stiff-legged down Gaston Avenue
for home, past the pawn shops and jukebox bars, where
we would sometimes crack a door and stare into the cool
dark, wanting to fall into it, be taken by it, as if willing
our futures to be.

To the west, a late day sun pooled on the skins
of new downtown skyscrapers. Some were still shapes,
unfinished puzzles of poured concrete and steel that peered
in disbelief (and later, resolve) over those shabby streets.

By the fall, I had moved to Chicago with my mother. He stayed
behind with my father, who took him out of East Dallas
to a subdivision north of the city, where new ranch homes
were trimmed with salvaged common brick from felled
buildings in cities like Toledo, Cleveland, and Detroit.
The years would pass, separated by conflicts and terrors
from wars we didn't start. Ragged skirmishes really,

though a boy couldn't tell. And a boy had to choose sides
to survive. We travelled into manhood as strangers

where I struggle to remember the names of his children,
who would not recall that afternoon on Gaston Avenue
when we shared the same wound, in a city
already forgetting we were there.

CS

SHIPWRECK

Past the river walk, where the water's edge
turns to dust and gravel, and the skyscrapers
seem as far away as money, a man who calls
this city his own suddenly feels small. The way
an Iowa kid must feel when he stands in the parking lot
of a shopping mall that was his family's farm
before he left for his college years.

The way a poet feels
when he thinks of the years before time
caught up with his home. Before the hotels
and luxury condominiums cast their empty shadows
on this staid river. Before the docks turned
into amusement parks lined with Ferris wheels
and gift shops, selling tiny porcelains
of the freighters and iron boats that used to anchor
in this harbor. Before the restaurants named
after fictitious widows of shipwrecks that never sank
here, but died the slow deaths of tired boats
and proud men whose hands grew calloused
with age and industry.

There was a city here, a city that cast pig iron,
built railroads, meat and refrigerators, shipped
jazz and trumpets, and the embryo of rock and roll
from the silent smile of a blues man's lips.

Writers celebrated its power, its swaggering,
boastful power, always spoiling for a fight,
another prairie, something to build.

From its breakfast table on Long Island, the world
called it crude, the ships squat and ugly, fit
only for those who could not sail, the music
vulgar, the women soiled, the men ignorant, the sky thick
with ash and despair.

And the city laughed, spitting soot and oil
from the gaps between its front teeth,
the city laughed.

A poet's job is to remember, he thinks
as he crushes out his cigarette on the new concrete
beneath him. The way Lydia McColleys lips felt
smooth, the way a rose petal feels smooth when it's found
in a sea of scrub weeds when he kissed her
for the first time under the Dearborn Street Bridge
in 1962, as the salt barges slid quietly by
in the October night.

The way the streets smelled like fish and oil,
the way the subways weren't called orange,
purple and green, but were named for streets
and neighborhoods: Jackson Park, Douglas Park,
Howard, Lake, Englewood. So that one had names
and history to help him make sense of his journeys.
The way nobody cared when the teen-teenagers
played on the rusted beaches at night, the way
town home developments with names like University Village
and Urban Manor wouldn't dare show their faces
on Halsted and Maxwell Streets, so that one could still get
lost there, wandering among the stolen hubcaps
and the smell of grilled onions.

It's been a long afternoon. His legs are tired
and he wonders how all of this happened,
the way and older man may wake in the night
reaching blindly for an image of himself
as a boy that left him moments before
in a dream. The way he catches colds easily now, falls
short of breath as he walks the iron staircase
to Upper Wacker Drive, how he's grown
tired of saying good-bye, to dread the sound
of an unringing phone.

There was a city here, he says to himself
as he steps out onto the street towards his hotel.
The last chords of daylight surrender noiselessly
behind the December sky. I remember now,
there was a city here.

CS

WEEKEND

aunt ree's house a lying dark rooms
of shadow finger of sun glints the plastic
couch cover its crinkle as much fixture
as cocoa the red cocker wearing chaotic
teeth & zoo smell living room sopped
in stench even hippy jesus on rock
above angry water holds his breath

now that stale whiskey & cheap beer
bang auntie's screen door cocoa
tracking scents leaps curled triangle
of outside ripped by boot or gust
under dining room arch adorned
in drab lilacs & dusky frames blonde
christ in varying salvations mama

dewy-eyed bone-tired sinless cowers
criespraysbegsscreamssheavyvexed
stuck behind aunt ree only dust settles
as daddy lunges left hand on flabby arm
right handles blade forged to shred beef
steel jabs air relentless profanity rage
alive on grungy shag saturday evening

outing cut short no electricity next
door pocket bulges aunt ree's *please*
petitions float from ceiling she sprawls
to floor & mama full with offspring
full with weary full with me spoiled
weekend gleam of knife in mama's
pupils a *stop* an *enough* a teenage hand

between shank and belly cousin mary
afro fist in mid-sixties southwest catches
skewer with palm tears a worryline
a lifeline another bloodline on the carpet
finger painting dusk by numbers
i make six i am seven months in
my siblings huddle in unforgiving black

BEING GOOD

In Kelly Park, a little boy wraps his arms
around his mother's legs as two girls come running
for his hill. The look in his eyes is part fear,
part curiosity. For his mother, it is one of those
moments that shape the collective sum of things,
an image made of many she may recall, an afternoon
in late September, her tremulous boy
holding on to the oak of her as she looks
across the dinner table at him twenty years later.
He has gone to Stanford. He is an engineer.

And so it is with memory, arriving in an instant
like this. His lank fingers down the front
of my sweatpants. His mustache, smelling
of fried eggs and nicotine, pressed against
my neck. Everything about him was old,
yet sheen, viscous like something dredged
from a dirty river that snakes through slag fields,
carrying coal barges down to the sea.

There was another boy there. While I have
not spoken to him in years, I want to
call him to say that one can trace a lifetime
of cowardice to a single moment, that Faulkner
was right about the past never being past,
that we should be careful of early autumn days
in our middle years, where everyday images
conflate into things we dare not see. That
I saw him there, in a treeless place
with me.

CS

WOOLWORTH'S POEM
for Russ and Tod

I.
we rode summer on ten speeds
bike routes to the courthouse lawn
where parking meter hitching posts
lined melting, technicolor days.

II.
we knew every corner
from the bird droppings in the basement
to the scent of musty popcorn.

III.
we laughed in the face of history.
him, golden locked and chubby nosed.
me, bubbling hot fudge.
we dared lunch counters innocently.
so close some thought us lovers.
we were.

IV.
the parakeets and canaries are no more.
silence creeps the arthritic escalator.
those fat, paisty, sandwich fingers
labor now in snaptight kitchens
across town, their tenderness lost.

V.

tod gave me a coffee mug
on the last day of business
before it became a museum.
he sat where freedom's students
wore ketchup and abuse
in a pre-jordan north carolina.
it is a simple mug.
opaque, speckled clay.
rounded handle.
sides geometrically balanced. sturdy.
it meant a lot to him
to give it to me.
it meant a lot to me to have it.

QAL

THE DAY RUSS DIED

after Frank O'hara

dark 4:30am sky buzzed alive
whatever birds sing that early
in brooklyn, discordant harmony
with clock nudge. hot water and towel

juice, vitamins, layers and coat, the corner
of east 46th street, dingy black town car
to utica. emerge forty minutes later from 4
train to odd still life. near campus, coffee

bagel, cinnamon-raisin from a bright
orange truck, long-haired bohemian
always chipper even in this frigid air
though manhattan knows little about winter.

steam from lips, students greet me in library
with poems, questions we mend. walk
to work at 10:30, the apple now spice
and sizzle. thursday, no class. 6 train to tribeca

hug sons at daycare, assemble
backpacks, outerwear. mama minutes later
in mini-van, angry streets, brooklyn
bridge, *which side to park today?* she wrestles

chicken, tofu, i splash naked boys, sculpt bubbles.
didn't hear it ring. when she calls me to dining room
sorrow is on our plates. hiking, he slid off table rock
dropped 85 feet, six waterfalls, body missing.

FOR HAZEL, MY GRANDFATHER'S MISTRESS

When Hazel died, my grandfather put on his boots,
waded through bush and briar patch to the place
where he chopped wood. He cut five halves
for a regular fire, at that time of year in North Carolina.
Then he rested against a wild oak tree,
took two breaths as he looked past a morning
sky, and died. Alone, save for the tired owls
and woodchucks who stayed up that morning
to watch the human heart break, to quietly surrender
to a symphony of September cicadas.

CS

46

HOMEMADE

i was made in st. stephens church
on choir pews behind an ageless pulpit.
under the almighty eye of mutha,
my cousins and i, led by aunties,
crafted stodgy hymns into poetry
with the love of God and song.

al green coloured saturday's song,
but flickering spirits painted church
sundays in deep human poetry.
our voices reached the oak pulpit,
then the small congregation, while aunties
bonnell and maudell stirred mutha

to rock and hum their gentle music. mutha
raised seven children on gospel song
and hard work. my mama, two uncles, & four aunties
talked with God in a tiny texas church
where an easy-tongued preacher stroked the pulpit,
sharing scripture as hereditary poetry.

between prayers they tilled poetry
with blood and sweat. in the garden, mutha
produced converts from her earthen pulpit:
stubborn tomatoes. melons ripe with tender song.
praising the hallowed floor of this church,
this land that knows my uncles and aunties

by name. led by my soulful aunties,
the family left calvert, texas to inspire poetry
a little further north. they found a church
home in a place called enid, then sent for mutha.
this tired soil, this birthplace of mama's song
was now a fond remembering, a lonely pulpit.

the space between preacher and pulpit
remains sacred. one of my aunties
now resides there, naturally. her song
full of light. her love like the poetry
of my sons' laughter. i feel mutha
everywhere. i know she's always church.

kneeling at church, i consider the pulpit,
dream about mutha and cherish my aunties.
a narrow rift divides poetry and song.

QAL

ALTAR CALL

I.
for brothas fathers husbands cousins
sons uncles nephews black manhood
in states of rebirth my teenage sons
groan to feet already half dreaming
food and football scores we stand
at rev's knees on red carpet at feet
of jesus beneath a twenty foot cross
with men we know and do not

scout leaders to the right (a confusion
i will never understand but have tried)
elders dressed sunday black men
carrying baby boys we place hands
on those by our sides bow

II.
i am at st. stephens a.m.e. swaddled
in thirty year old acned paneling
pews creak familiar mildewed
dustrag of flag between railing
and empty organ my cousins
near we are youth xmas show
easter pageant choir concert

i am looking for the church fan
family long to be flawless boy godly
teeth scripture by heart it never opens

III.
in a corner in a room
in a heart there is a door

through the door in a room
in a heart is a corner
turn the corner in a room

in the heart there is a door

through the door in a corner
there is a room in a heart

meet me there we will make
room in the corner for our hearts

IV.

i call them close wrap arms
around my selves share words
never uttered in childhood

after service we rouse youngest
winterize for city streets all hungry
and morning an anxious night

V.

attended church with daddy twice
both were funerals one was his

QAL

50

CHICAGO

East Texas, split barbed wire
on the side of Mr. Pickerings's pasture. Two spent steer
chewing dandelions and dirt. My brother
and me cutting our backs on trench posts
because we wanted to break into something
that broiling summer. We'd be run out of here
soon enough, tumble out of town
in a rented truck, my mother jittery
for the anonymity of the interstate. Northbound on I-35
until we ran out of borders, and all that was left
were the refineries on Ogden Avenue, and the grey
lights of a northern skyline built with the last lathes
of American steel in the years before anyone thought
it would shimmer again. She talked us in
to Travelodge on Sheridan Road, fell asleep
for weeks to chase the nightmares away,
woke us up with subway tokens and vague directions
to explore. Roared our way
all the way to 135th Street. Even the cops
said welcome home.

CS

IV.

ROUTINE

every evening after the six o'clock
i ate dinner, something fast, sitting
at the desk. eight tv screens, three police
scanners talking to themselves
ears keen to chatter i'd not heard
earlier. check news radio at top of hour
just dry heat. then phones — seven pm
roll call — public information officers
at eight village precincts. *nothing*
goin on but a bunch of darkies drinkin
in del city. i am certain of his skin
secure inside the box, babylon's mouth
the lead story at ten, willie horton, sundowner
law still dripping. *you are talking to one.*
next day, managing editor assaults
his superior, attends while information
officer phones in apology.

QAL

STATEMENT ON THE KILLING OF PATRICK DORISMOND

a petty hoodlum (cop) shot/killed suspect (blackman) after
hoodlum (pig) was told by suspect (haitian) that he
(junglebunny) was not a drug dealer (nigga). the police
commissioner (bounty hunter) referred to suspect (coon) as a
"lowlife" (african) though his (aryan) comments were later
proven false (white lies). the shooting (genocide) is the third
(pattern) in thirteen months (institution) in which plain-
clothes officers (gestapo) shot/killed an unarmed man (cheap
blood). "I would urge (doubletalk) everyone (oprah) not to
jump (dead nigga) to conclusions (acquittals)," mayor guiliani
(watchdog) said, "and allow (blind faith) the facts (ethnic
cleansing) to be analyzed (spin) and investigated (puppets)
without people (darkies) trying to let their biases (racial
profiling), their prejudices (welfare queen), their emotions
(fuck tha police), their stereotypes (o.j.) dictate the results
(status quo)."

QAL

OBITUARY

for Alice Marie Smith

1.
Those of your kind that are left will line
the pews at First Presbyterian in blue Chanel
suits that hang from their spindly bodies
like Old Glory on a windless January day.
They will cough politely, be assisted
by their sixty year old children, cry
tears of dust and aerosol.

2.
1942. His P-47 falls into the ocean. He writes
from a field hospital in Samoa. The atoll was
shark infested, his face and chest
hammered into the pull stick, blood
and the rest of it left behind as he crawls
from his wrecked ship. A long, soundless
night save for the tumble of the sea and his
chanting the sweetheart's name he gave you
at Lake Texoma in the summer of '39. It kept him
alive. He left a son with you. You would see
his face there. And you would seethe.

3.
The Reverend Tyler Johnson officiate, but you will direct.
The local mortician will do you up nice, pry
the last smirk from your lips, fold your lank fingers
over a frigid patch of skin where your heart
used to be. There will be thin eulogies that dissolve
in the air above the rafters. Your curriculum
vitae will be read between the lines of names
and places like Gate City, Virginia, United Daughters
of the Confederacy, Order of the Eastern Star,
Daughters of the American Revolution.
No one in that fearful crowd will afford the irony

of a woman so vainglorious of her ancestry,
yet so repulsed by those
whose ancestry she will be.

4.
1967. You sent toy guns for Christmas.
My mother threw them away.
Tet the following year.

5.
1991. We met once, you and me. At my father's funeral.
We shook hands. *We shook hands*. The sum total
of us.

6.
When November comes in North Texas
not so much as a quail will stir around your grave.
Toss a hand of dry dirt over the coffin, boys.
watch it sift over the cool mahogany,

and fall away.
Nothing ever grew there.
Nothing ever will.

CS

RUBBLE
for Mrs. Clara Luper

My biggest job now is making white people understand that black history is white history. We cannot separate the two.
                    -Clara Luper, Associated Press interview, 2006

I.
dear mrs. luper

i knew you before that atlanta
preacher you were closer to home dirt
red from men sent to texas burdened
with mid june words fed a girlchild

in okfuskee county who understood jesus
was not inside a hospital that kept her sick
brother out the house near hammon
held together by a maid and brickworker

folk who ached their bones brittle
in august heat faith grown smile
a mask & truth *daddy said someday will be
real soon* tears long as endless walking

and as hope greenwood one hour
& three minutes on seventy-five fourteen
years of kingdom building ashes
in seventy two hours two years before love

& mercy birthed you here on this
god trembled land this almost native
this almost black this almost right
rooted in possibility and far-sighted

promise you put on those cat-eye
glasses to see yesterday today
and that a young child can lead
if she knows what is required

II.
twelve children three adults & you
at katz dressed in courage and spittle
the nation yawned okies awoke
six months and a year pre-greensboro

daddy never able to sit down and eat
a meal in a decent restaurant history
compels us to go let history alone
be our final judge state law upheld

your twenty six handcuffings twenty six
cellblocks twenty six steel wool blankets
twenty six concrete nights twenty six
are the children safe twenty six

i want to sleep in my bed

not everyone sat with you mrs. luper
legislated fear and lynching bees
men provide or don't john tubman
didn't think harriet was coming back either

like her, justice work and prayer filled your empty

III.
you said *if christianity fails then we surrender* perhaps it has
mrs. luper more likely we have stumbled on the path
still in rubble and debris we pray we are the center
you built with worn giving hands a slight remembering
of what was   a clear light on what remains to be done

sincerely

your son in progress

QAL

POVERTY (IN THE LIBRARY LOBBY)

She is a dangle of waiting, this little girl.
Stone-faced in a grubby tee-shirt
and too small gym shoes as her mother hollers
over the pay phone at the electric company, the landlord,
the last man who walked out on her,
the way

my sisters and me shivered the shame
of the same public scene in out grown clothes
while my mother shouted down ex-husbands and bad debt
in motel lobbies off state roads the interstates left
behind, discount store return desks, truck stops,
food stamp offices.

It gets better, child. I know how
you hate yourself this morning. But when
you remember, you will count the thin blessing
of humiliations in front of strangers. Later,
they will become useful things, like a flashlight
in a cluttered basement where we store things
we never use, but always need.

But for now, her chocolate eyes meet mine:
Keep it moving, mister.
Nothing to see here.

CS

61

ELEGY

for Gwendolyn Brooks

I.
twelve years ago, met
chitown with $25, two suitcases
and a folder of poems, in search
of myself. you, haki and malcolm
had knocked enough red dirt
from my eyes to see black.

II.
i have seen your words
change rural fourth graders
into southside pool toughs
hustling jazz in june

III.
in class, you ignited riots
watched us loot and ransack.

IV.
at dinner, your mortality
stiffened me, forced to consider
this in your absence, sobered
by the bone of your words.

QAL

KLAN MARCH

perhaps in a sincere gesture of protest
the managing editor decided it best
i welcome the grand imperial wizard
to channel nine, guide him back to
the senior producer's glass cube
where he would proceed to engage
in heated words with the general
manager, whose robe hung upstairs
on the executive suite door. neither
of us offered our hands. staffers gathered
around me at the desk for a better view
of the meeting, questioned the cause
for vein pop and venom bleed
through office walls, summer sun
redefining our faces.

QAL

AFTERNOON IN EAST HUMBOLDT

Someone nailed a milk crate to the phone pole,
hammered a piece of plywood on the back
so the north block kids got a round ball goal
in the alley. It's a place on the map

for a pee wee hoop less than six feet high
So the neighborhood enforces the rules.
You wont see warriors over five feet try
dribbling here opposite some shorty fool.

It's left for the first and second graders
who arrive after school, in the sweet hours
between Corduroy and the deal makers
I've watched them become. Campbell Street's power:

hawking loose rocks while the concrete ages
beneath them, history turns the pages.

CS

WALLACE

A man follows his shadow along the east wall of the Lincoln
Memorial. A cardboard sign the size of a piece of typing paper
hangs from his neck, over a dirty yellowing tee-shirt that lays
over his chest. The message is written in faded blue marker. It
says: "You're closer than you think." It is a Tuesday morning
and the crowd is light. A few dozen tourists holding
camcorders form a line along the south wall, waiting for the
gift shop to open.

I stand about two feet behind him, moving my lips along with
the words from the Second Inaugural, skinny and afraid of the
world, just beginning to learn the promise of what language
can bring. My eyes racing like sparrows that morning to Billy
Henderson, who stood slumped shouldered at Lincoln's feet,
who stalked me that day through museums and libraries with
an ease that told him we never left home, that this place was as
familiar for him as the parking lot behind the Becker Junior
High School gym, who would beat me later in Room 307 of the
Americana Hotel as my roommate watched. "Fucking pussy,"
he grunted as he worked his thick fists over my kidneys.
Chunks of spittle pooled in the corner of his lips. "Think you're
so god-damned smart. You can't hide from me."

"My name is Wallace," says the homeless man as he turns
suddenly and faces me, stirring up the air enough for me smell
the street on his clothes, "and a man ain't nothing if he don't
have a name." He turns his body to face the crowd waiting in
front of the gift shop. "And let me tell you, brothers and sisters,
that you gotta have an opinion of you gonna make it in this
town. And my opinion is this: the best nation is a donation!"
He pulls a decaying McDonalds coffee cup from an ancient
Washington Post newspaper bag he wears on his side, smiles
broadly and begins walking towards a middle-aged man in a
Florida Marlins cap, who quickly looks away. "Anything will
help, brothers and sisters," he continues. The crowd inches

closer to the wall. "Anything will help. I'm 100 percent tax deductible!"

It was a late flight. The 757 circled the snow clouds over Wilmington for an hour before touching down in Baltimore to find us. We shuffled down the jet bridge like weary prisoners. We reached altitude over western Maryland, and the cabin filled with the uneven rhythm of keyboards.

A college student follows the flight attendant with his eyes until he grows tired, turns his head towards the window and finds his sleep staring into the night.

Maybe it was the hour. Maybe it was the way the jetliner tunneled through the shadows above the storm clouds, or the way the low, even hum of the starboard engine could lull us into something like sleep in the air over West Virginia. A tablet computer slips from the hands of a businessman in 26B. His head sinks slowly to his shoulder in surrender. His mouth falls open and he begins to dream.

A software engineer in 23C fingers lay still over her keyboard as her eyes begin to close. Her head falls back, and struggles against it for moment. Her hair pours over her face in waves. "My husband's name is Michael," she told me as we waited at the gate, her breath sticky with vodka and tonic. Her lips moved with slow deliberation, scooping each word from her mouth like a spoon to a chocolate sundae. "He works at Motorola in network assurance. You may know him. He does a lot of work with your university. He's a prick."

Two stockbrokers repeat the same questions to each other in the 19th row until they stop pretending to listen and fall wordlessly back into their seats.

And then another, and another, until we all sleep as if drugged with fatigue, and there is no sound in the cabin except for the even hum of a starboard engine, which even them seemed far away in the sky over Pennsylvania.

I dreamed of Frenchmen and hockey games, of libraries with shelves lined with the remains of charred dictionaries, of broken cardboard boxes drifting like tumbleweed down M Street. I saw the faces of my forefathers drinking whisky in a North Texas rainstorm, laughing as the cotton fields lay fallow. I heard the thousand words about DC and the voices that filled them: a young woman in a green housecoat having a conversation with the sidewalk at the steps of the National Gallery. A wanderer who weeps quietly to himself as he finds a name on a panel of the Vietnam Memorial. An old man pushing a grocery cart down Pennsylvania Avenue, filled with aluminum cans, empty milk cartons, and other remains of other people's days. The musician who sings Little Milton songs to the rush hour commuters at the subway entrance in Dupont Circle as they disappear down the escalator like field mice burrowing down for another long winter. The street people sleeping atop the heating grates in front of the FBI Building.

A group of office workers eating cottage cheese plates at the Justice Department cafeteria, whispering their lover's secrets in each other's ears. The constant sound of helicopters landing on rooftops. The blue shadows of armor plated limousines moving like ghosts in the grey dawn down Massachusetts Avenue. The twisted symphony of sirens always in the distance.

There is a moment before a jetliner lands. The turbines idle in the seconds before the wheels touch ground, and the aircraft seems suspended. It is a moment of indescribable peace. It is over as soon as it begins. The rear gears hit the tarmac with a soft thud, reverse thrust engages, and we wake. When the plane reaches the gate, we gather our things as children would. We walk through the terminal as we began, silent and alone, our minds already filling with the minutiae of tomorrow's American morning, of line items and 8:30 meetings, of the strict cadence of schedules that keep us one step ahead of things we cannot name. A storm breaks in the Northeast. What's left of its fury heads out to sea and dissipates in the stratosphere. We round the corner for baggage claim, our eyes squinting into the coming light.

Wallace leaves by the west steps and heads north into the night. He stops to tie his shoe at the banks of the reflecting pool. A helicopter passes overhead.

CS

WILL ROGERS TURNPIKE

these roads my veins dry red
clay body sun smoke wafts heat
tired of itself wheezing semi-trailers
alfalfa between cheek and gum

cicada guitar twang ditties tink
powerline towers alien horizon
march shoulders hawk respite
in absence of elm and birch

dust devils square dance prairie
as christian clouds loft fervor
sun to our right only sky blue
this land our road hum and scent

something dead every quarter mile
what are you, mexican? the kind cracker
asks at truck stop amazed to learn
of duet between nelly and tim mcgraw

patience is the i-35 junction abrupt
urban merger   night a blindfold
headlights on city
licks chops and growls

QAL

V.

SUNDAY AT MUTHA'S

Boy, don't you kick that ball in tha garden. If you kick that
ball in tha garden one mo time, imma tan yo' little brown hiney.
—Anna "Mutha" Lawrence

we could hardly wait for crusty ol' reverend
jenkins' final *Amen* so the real sunday
afternoon could commence.

fried chicken and fresh catfish.
aunt maudell's potato salad.
aunt bonnell's cakes.

fresh corn on the cob and green
beans from mutha's garden.

more than a plot of plowed soil, this was
community center, where her children worked
sad earth, where her grandkids destroyed it fifty yards away.

she sat on the sagging porch, lifted
by four high cinder blocks, to watch the sabbath unfold.

almost unholy how worship affects
young black appetites but my cousins and me
were squirming in choir pews for one reason.
wasn't the holy spirit or soul food

it was kickball. no game ever completed. always
some form of tragedy--pam skinning up her knee,
chucky throwing the ball hard upside rae's head

or losing skipper to the kitchen. he ate
everything. all the time. once he made a salad
dressing sandwich on white bread.

man, that's some nasty stuff.
you a samwich eatin' meathead emptyshoe!

another time in the kitchen two nieces
and a nephew were covered from head
to toe in chocolate. it was ex-lax.

fear upon entering mutha's bathroom.
sometimes the light chain stuck.
pulling, trying to hit the stool, because
you knew a whuppin' was coming
if you missed. an old maple traced the window.

the inside of your pants warm and sticky.

when mutha joined the ancestors
jaybird moved into her house
front porch supported by the same
cement squares. cousins jaybird, chucky and i
sitting around chilling. it didn't feel right.
but i wasn't afraid to use the toilet.

QAL

THE WILL ROGERS TURNPIKE

Having a soda on a temperate day
while I watch my mind float to another place.

A waitress fondles trucker music with her wiry, spellbound
ears as I leave this scene,
letting the syrupy real thing make me all warm inside,
freeing my blood to the suburbs of my neurosis.

Back on the interstate where the armadillos,
through an uncommon twist of fate,
are flattened in the early morning sun.

I scream past them,
catching a quick, curious glance at the flies eating
away at their souls.

The waitress is back on the screen,
her "beef, real food for real people" thighs wrapped
around my vegetarian throat.

She chokes me for awhile,
whispering in a rayon voice that I never had it like this.

Two burly, farting truckers laugh at me,
picking the okra from their teeth as they shit in the
dingy caverns of suppressed homosexuality.

My divorced parents celebrate on a waterbed,
bought on sale at a shopping mall built over an old
armadillo farm.

Back in Wisconsin, exiled liberals refinish overpriced
antique love seats,
cursing Geraldo Rivera's mustache and other mass media
hypocrisies while their children watch Sesame Street
at gunpoint.

The car is moving faster now,
past the armadillos
into an art bar where it's fashionable to be depressed
and secretly dream of portable furniture.

A rock hard, boot cut colonel makes me pee in a room
next to a thousand snickering, volunteer army GIs . . .

And all I can do is stare,
wishing I were in a street slickened, playful graffiti
benefit concert sort of way.

And I long for the Great Southwest,
where I could sit in a restaurant surrounded by Mary Kay
porno queens eating fruit salad plates.

Mounds and mounds of fruit salad plates and nowhere
to take them.

The car is moving faster now,
past the exits to the small, not so sleepy towns where
everyone eats Oreida frozen fish sticks and like Roman
candy store owners pour onto the high school football
fields on Friday nights, sucking in the autumn air while
they spit on tradition and secretly masturbate to images
of white supremacists knawing on beeflivers in a cross
burning camp outside of Salt Lake City.

I know, I used to live in that town.

The car is moving faster now,
and I'm maintaining an optimal altitude while a sultry,
love me for my body not my mind stewardess serves me
some processed cheese spread.

And my mind wanders to the bed of a seventeen year old
with a rich grandmother,
my ego being stocked while I admire my jawline.

But she's out of my life now,
pumped through the millions of neon lit make up room to
the immortality of Southern California.
Dancing through endless hours of impotent plastic surgeon/
slumlords who fantasize about having mulatto children
with the inner city women who give them the respect they
so badly deserve?

"You can get off anywhere or anytime you want," says
the stewardess as she molds my uneaten cheese spread
into GI Joe meets Barbie action figures.

I'm back on the Westside now,
sitting in an eighteen hour workday Mexican bar listening
to Hispanic renditions of Barry Manilow tunes, thinking
of Castro doing a rumba on Hemingway's old Cuban estate
while Papa bossman blows his worldly wise, Nobel Prize
winning brains out in an Idaho potato field just before
someone took that really creepy picture of little
John John Kennedy, fully clad in designer deathware,
giving one last good American lobster fed salute to
his gravebound father and I don't know why but I always
feel sick when I look at that picture . . .

My truck stop vixen, back from a commercial break, didn't
have to tell me that I had made a big mistake coming
to a place that, like any late night seventies sitcom
subculture, never really bothered me, but never really
left me alone

She comforted me,
holding me in her almost masculine but not yet tattooed
arms and told me that everything was OK and that I could
move with her to Tulsa if I wanted

Where later we'd sit in the early morning sun,
having safe sex in our freeze dried decaffinated ranch
home bedroom, feeding Rice Chex to our armadillo children
who unlike their father would never
never,
ever,
go anywhere near

an interstate.

CS

HIGHER ED
a found poem

Division of Continuing Education
Administration, Supervision & Collaboration:
Moving to the Next Level
Friday, March 26
Canceled

QAL

MEMORANDUM
AD HOC COMMITTEE ON OFFICE ASSIGNMENTS

the assignment of offices in the department is limited to regular faculty division membership and determined by levels of melanin and estrogen. regular faculty division membership is defined by belonging to the hannity and colmes social club. seniority is arrived at by the following point system based on decaying penises and viagra levels. faculty members will be ordered by the total number of racist and sexist commentary accrued over their total number of years served as regular faculty division members. the total number of points is the sum of the product of the negative sperm count in each rank and the yearly points of that count. ties will be broken by the following: first by degree of unwarranted arrogance, second by measure of debilitating insecurity, and third by most ancient publication date.

rank	number of points per rank
all people of color who are not white males	-0
all others who are not white males	1
white males	3

QAL

THE CONVERT

When they started tearing down the Berlin Wall, you
were in bed with an Irish girl, fumbling through
half-filled ashtrays, wine glasses, and smudged
manuscripts for a condom. In the next room
you can hear the muffled voice of a well dressed
American reporter, live from the Brandenburg Gate
where thousands of ruddy cheeked East Germans wave
cigarette coupons, bibles, and Buy-Rite tickets as signs
of their newfound freedom. It was here that Henry IV stood
barefoot in the snow for three days, pleading
for Pope Gregory to lift his excommunication, while you
waited in the Leipzig airport, fighting boredom
with over-priced ice cream bars and endless hours
of Teutonic daydreams. The French are scared. Nestle stands
to make some money. Henry goes on to capture Rome
and Pope Gregory dies in exile, as you
explode together in orgasm. Another victory

for the Free World.

CS

SUSPENDED IN ANIMATION

hey, hey, hey! where are you?
we've got some work to do
now. here i come to save the day.
whenever he gets in a fix, he reaches
into his bag of tricks.

kill the wabbit? but that trick never works.
this time for sure we'd a gotten away
with it, if it hadn't a been
for those meddling kids. you're despicable.

heavens to mergatroid, jane.
please stop this crazy thing.

QAL

SONNET FOR THE INNOCENTS
at Gaylord Opryland® Resort and Convention Center, Nashville, Tennessee

There is no weather here. Man made perch ponds
guide lift ramps and the faithful to the prize
of bric-a-brac bayou. Haitian maids don
antebellum dresses, curtsy replies,

and we would beg clemency for our sins,
redemption at the Delta Island Food Court
to make meaning of this garden we tend,
had simple fortune not made us the sort

who exchange solace for indoor rivers
with no current, and no destination.
Hank Williams is a rumor delivered
by those who would ransom our salvation

and drop a sad, lonely note in this crowd.
Perhaps. If only a mess were allowed.

CS

BROWN SUGAR

Saturday afternoon, wandering north on Ashland in a rented
Hyundai—lilac, with no acceleration and no tape player.
Because of the former, I was running late for the poetry
reading of two close friends. Because of the latter, I was
heavily occupied with frequency exploration. After a few
commercials, a plea for my salvation and a little Hootie (which
can be too much Hootie, depending on one's state of being) the
radio selector landed on the final yelps of Led Zepplin's "Dyer
Maker". I lingered for a moment, troubled the first three
minutes eluded me. I remembered something that came to me
in 1985, during my tenure at the University of Oklahoma. In a
hazy mind state, I announced to my homeboys, *Black folks
created rock and roll. The only thing white folks contributed that even
made a difference was smack.* It's true, but damn was I self-
righteous, I'm thinking, when the chords to "Brown Sugar"
kick in. Such a timeless piece of art from those Rolling Stones.
My head began to bob without thought, like groove had been
buried there. Russ, my closest Oklahomey, discovered the Hot
Rocks album our senior year of high school. On any Friday
night in 1982, you might spot him atop a pump jack, a beer in
one hand, pump jack in the other, pouting lips while yelping *I
can't get no . . . satisfaction.* Though, I was the girly action-less
one. *I'm no schoolboy, but I know what I like. You shoulda heard em
just around midnight.* It's summer following my first year at OU,
and I'm back at my parent's house. Camp counselor by day,
restless by night. One evening the phone rang and my father
answered. "It's for you," he grunted, aiming the receiver my
way. "Hello . . . hello . . . ," and it's Mick's voice, *Brown Sugar,
how come ya do it so good, yeah. Brown Sugar, just like a young girl
should, yeah.* "Hello?"But, it's only Mick. Only the chorus to
Brown Sugar. For three months, often four times a week. That
was the last summer I lived with my parents. My head's
bobbin' on automatic, like this car's transmission, still cruising
north on Ashland keeping time with Keith Richards' licks. A
college friend once told me Keith invented heroin. I believed

him. I still do. Damn, I could've made that light, as the red pickup meanders across Lake Street. I check my watch. Damn, it's a quarter to two. I look to my right, and there's Garrett Morris at the bus stop. I pull over, roll down the passenger window, and ask if he wants a ride. He grins, glassy eyes sagging, and joins me. He says he's out looking for the women Mick ponders in the song. I tell him that skit has always been a favorite of mine and we converse about the current sorry state of Saturday Night Live. He jets at Chicago Avenue, promising to phone me when he finds these women. Mick's preparing to wrap it up. At that very moment, a revelation: Just *who* is he talkin' about? Is he talkin' about my Great Grandmother, who wore slavery in the wrinkle of her back, yet still held Jim Crow at gunpoint for 99 years? Or my Grandmother, who cleaned up behind drunken country and western singers and their one night lovers at the Roadside Motel? Is he talkin' bout my niece Whitnee, who, at eleven, is the same age as Pocahontas when she met John Smith? Whitnee, who has never brought home anything lower than an A on any report card in her life? Is he talkin' bout my mama? My sistas? My aunties? My cousins? My wife? Don't go there, Mick. *Just like a . . . just like a Black Girl should.* My head stopped bobbing. I pressed the scan button with a great sense of urgency. Toni Braxton in mid ooze, *The very thought of you makes me wanna get undressed...* I screamed, prayed for my car's speedy recovery and turned off the radio. I was late to the reading.

QAL

MISSISSIPPI RIVER AT THE NEW ORLEANS CRESCENT

Big ass Panamanian freighter,
a ballast of cocaine and human traffic.
A busy port knows no natives.
All of us just passing through.

Jean Lafitte at Pierre Maspero's Exchange,
narking on the British at Chalmette.
Artillery, iron guns, troop positions, news of
the Welsh commander, who receives notice of his Louisiana
commission as he poses languidly for an officer's portrait
in a Sheffield drawing room. A red coat courier delivers
the news, adding Godspeed, incept dates, the name of
a waiting ship, and the surety of a defeated hillbilly army
at the mouth of the Mississippi.

The half finished portrait hangs on a south wall
at the English National Gallery, gathering dust
and the occasional tourist's question: "Who was
Pakenham?," whose troops waited in the tall grass
behind the Rodriguez Canal, shipped out after Waterloo,
one-upping each other with stories of dead Frenchman
and rumors of Napoleon's exile to New Orleans.
Two thousand of them died in thirty minutes,
cut down in a sugar cane field
by a conscripted Tennessee brigade, whose ferocity
was matched only by their desire to return home, to leave
this place, the sick heat of it, the side deals,
the foreign languages.

Jackson raises a glass with him, pays him
in shiny American silver, and the freedom to do as he pleases
in New Orleans. Lafitte didn't need permission.
He'd been trading Africans at the Chartres Street Armory
for decades, as he would for decades more.
He wanted to die a patriot.
And so he did.

The passport says, "do as you please."
Father Antione's alabaster eyes
stare down from the cathedral garden.
"Only in sin can one know its rival in redemption."

We take Lafitte with us down Rue Dauphine.
"Listen to the walls," I say to Gordon.

"I don't hear anything."

"The wages of sin," Gordon bellows, "is more sin!"

Gordon's good at counting things, makes a living
pruning pennies from other people's pockets.
When he's drunk, he likes to add it all up:
his second mortgage, the beer soaked dollar bills
he slides into the stripper's g-string at Big Daddy's
("wash the girl of your choice"), his college-aged daughter
(who he says has already outlived him), his first wife
(who he says makes coffee nervous). Later, she hustles us
for a 20 dollar table dance, drags a plywood box
scuffed with agency to the back of the room, where
we tap our thin feet to an 80s R&B tune, so close
(he says he can smell the honey of her).

Back home, time ticks
in the suburban Midwest,
nothing is negotiable
and it always three in the afternoon.

Jean Lafitte is a hero of the Republic.
All of us just passing through.

CS

CLARK STREET SONNET

There are myriad paths to memory.
One is winter, driving north on Clark Street
on a February night, mysteries
rising from the pavement like steam, to greet

me where I grew, howling the alleyways
and other jagged places, secret maps
of these neighborhoods, where I gladly paid
the bargain price of youth, in a basement flat

with a dime bag and luck. We groped out loud
though we knew the place was changing, in pursuit
of new gentry, condos, a monied crowd
in us, around us, emptying of youth.

Yet these streets stayed with me, what I became,
still in the shadows, reinventing the game.

CS

Author Photo © Leilondi McCoy | Harmony Photography

About the Poets

Quraysh Ali Lansana is author of seven poetry books, three textbooks, a children's book, editor of eight anthologies, and coauthor of a book of pedagogy. He is Associate Professor of English/Creative Writing at Chicago State University, where he served as Director of the Gwendolyn Brooks Center for Black Literature and Creative Writing from 2002-2011. *Our Difficult Sunlight: A Guide to Poetry, Literacy & Social Justice in Classroom & Community* (with Georgia A. Popoff) was published in March 2011 by Teachers & Writers Collaborative and was a 2012 NAACP Image Award nominee. Lansana's poetry collection *mystic turf* was released in October 2012 by Willow Books; his most recent collection of poems, *reluctant minivan,* was published in May 2014 by Living Arts, Tulsa.

Christopher Stewart's poetry has appeared in numerous poetry journals and the anthology, *Power Lines: A Decade of Poetry* from Chicago's Guild Complex. His collaborations with music artists include his work with the group Circadian Rhythm, which was featured on the audio anthology, *A Snake in the Heart: Poems and Music* by Chicago Spoken Word Performers. He is an assistant professor in the Graduate School of Library and Information Science at Dominican University.

CPSIA information can be obtained
at www.ICGtesting.com
Printed in the USA
FFOW02n2127280115
10653FF